A fundamental assumption in public finance is that individuals consider taxes when making economic choices. There is indeed a voluminous literature showing that taxes significantly influence behaviors along several margins including labor supply, portfolio allocations, and savings.[1] Under the standard interpretation, these behavioral responses are attributed to changes in marginal tax rates (MTR), assuming that individuals understand the tax schedule that they face. However, there are numerous sources of complexity in U.S. federal income tax code, and learning the details of tax provisions can be costly in terms of cognitive effort, time and money. These costs may lead some taxpayers to remain unaware of tax provisions that currently affect them, or that will affect them in the future. A recent and growing literature on tax salience suggests that complexity of the income tax system may complicate the ability of taxpayers to fully understand their tax-induced incentives. As a result, misperceptions over the tax system may importantly influence behavioral responses to tax policy.

This paper offers two contributions to the literature on taxpayer perceptions of the tax system. Our first contribution is that we develop a model that generates predictions over how taxpayers update their beliefs about their marginal tax rates when they experience an unexpected change in their tax liability. Our model is an extension of a standard full-information, rational agent model that allows for imperfect knowledge of the income tax schedule. In the model, a household is subject to a linear tax schedule that changes from year to year. The household perceives innovations to the tax schedule with noise due to information gathering and processing costs. When the household is uncertain about the exact tax schedule it faces, it updates its beliefs using signals about the tax schedule generated by interactions with the tax system. The model predicts that when a surprisingly

---

[1]See, for example, Eissa (1995) or Eissa and Liebman (1996) for labor force participation of women, Looney and Singhal (2006) for the intertemporal elasticity of labor earnings, Goolsbee (2000) for the timing of income realization, Poterba and Samwick (2003) for risk-taking and portfolio behavior, and Feldstein (1995), Auten and Carroll (1999), Gruber and Saez (2002), and Kopczuk (2005) for reported and taxable income. On the other hand, Saez (2004) finds that only the top 1% of incomes show evidence of behavioral responses to taxation.

2

high (low) tax liability is perceived, the household updates its beliefs about the current and future MTRs upwards (downwards). This updating occurs even when changes in tax liability are perfectly predictable well in advance.

Our second contribution is that we devise an empirical strategy that allows us to test whether households fully internalize their tax schedule changes or whether they misperceive predictable changes in tax liability that they experience. As a source of identifying variation, we use the age-discontinuity in eligibility for the Child Tax Credit (CTC) at the age of 17. Importantly, the change in tax liability due to the loss of the credit is lump-sum, predictable in advance, and arguably exogenous. We examine how this variation affects household labor income for married-couple households whose child turns 17 just before the end of a year (and who therefore lose the credit) to their counterparts whose child turns 17 early in the following year (and who therefore do not yet lose the credit). Because this variation is lump-sum and predictable, barring liquidity constraints, there should be no reaction in labor supply and labor income in response to the loss of the credit. However, if parents misperceive the source of this tax liability increase, our model predicts that they will erroneously believe that part of this increase was due to an increase in their marginal tax rates.

As with many other aspects of the federal income tax code, the rules for CTC eligibility are complex. It would therefore not be surprising if taxpayers were confused over its administration.[2] The President's Advisory Panel on Federal Tax Reform (2005) reports:[3]

> "To determine something as basic as figuring out the tax implications of
> having a child, you need to review numerous rules and complete many separate
> sets of computations. Figuring out whether you can claim the child tax credit,

---

[2]A frequent counter argument is that computer tax software minimizes the need to work through the complexity in order to file taxes. We feel that this only strengthens the arguments put forth in this paper as the taxpayer is allowed to be even more uniformed as to how certain events impact his tax obligations and overall turns the tax system into a black box.

[3]In "Simple, Fair, and Pro-Growth: Proposals to Fix America's Tax System", a report of the President's Advisory Panel on Federal Tax Reform, November 2005. Source: www.taxreformpanel.gov.

for example, requires the skills of a professional sleuth: You need to complete eight lines on a tax form, perform up to five calculations, and fill out as many as three other forms or schedules. Further research, reading, and computation may be needed to determine whether you can claim head of household filing status, an exemption for a dependent, the child and dependent care credit, the earned income tax credit, or tax credits related to your child's education, to name only some of the possibilities."

To implement our empirical design, we construct a panel from the universe of U.S. federal tax returns filed between 2001 and 2008. We estimate that losing an eligible dependent for the CTC significantly reduces the growth rate of household labor income following the loss of the credit. This result is obtained even though losing the CTC has no mechanical impact on MTRs for most households. We argue that the finding cannot be driven by the presence of liquidity constraints because these constraints would imply a higher, rather than lower, growth rate of labor income for households who lose the credit. We interpret this result as due to taxpayer misperceptions regarding the nature of tax changes that are experienced. Using a generally acceptable range of elasticity estimates from the labor supply literature, our estimates suggest that households misinterpret more than half of the increased tax liability as due to a change in MTR. To our knowlege, our results present the first systematic evidence using administrative data that households not only misinterpret perfectly predictable tax changes but act upon those misperceptions as well.

Our results are robust to several alternative explanations. We show that our findings are not driven by a direct effect of child aging or a spurious correlation between the timing of birth and income growth. We also find similar results when we exclude households where children in the treatment and control groups are likely to be in different academic grades due to state-based school enrollment policies. The robustness checks further imply that the CTC has no significant effect on the growth rate of household labor income in the years

4

before its loss, suggesting that the effect is not driven by a strategic retiming of income realizations.

Our empirical analysis contributes to the literature on tax salience in several ways. First, much of the empirical analysis of tax salience occurs in an experimental setting (e.g., Chetty et al. (2009); Hossain and Morgan (2006); and Feldman and Ruffle (2013)). Second, administrative tax return data provides a relatively large sample of households to examine and permits us to credibly identify valid treatment and control groups. A small number of other studies have been able to examine tax salience issues using administrative data, however, these studies tend to focus on choices other than labor supply (e.g., Turner (2011)) or focus on low-income households (e.g., Chetty et al. (forthcoming)). Lastly, many studies in this literature use variation in the salience or framing of a tax parameter and examine whether this variation affects individual choices. We take a different approach by examining responses to a change in tax liability to infer whether a tax policy is correctly perceived. Our approach offers a methodology for examining tax salience issues in settings where changing the degree of salience is not possible.

Our finding that taxpayers misperceive even perfectly predictable tax liability changes has important implications for tax policy. In particular, estimates of the behavioral responses to tax policy that are obtained when one assumes that taxpayers respond to the actual source of a tax liability change will under- or over-estimate the elasticities of interest if taxpayers instead respond to a misperceived change in tax policy. Our theoretical model infoms the relative magnitudes of actual and perceived changes in marginal tax rates, and thus, the direction of bias imparted onto these elasticity estimates. Understanding the relationship between misperceptions about tax policy and the resulting behavioral responses to taxes informs how taxpayers interact with the tax system.

# 1  Related Literature

There is a literature in public finance that analyzes how well-informed taxpayers are about the tax system that they face. One strand of this literature focuses on documenting taxpayer perceptions of the income tax schedule. Brown (1968) compares self-reported MTRs of a group of UK taxpayers to their actual MTRs computed out of employer pay records and concludes that taxpayers "think they pay higher rates of tax than is in fact the case." Fujii and Hawley (1988), using the Survey of Consumer Finances, compare respondent self-reported MTRs to estimates of these MTRs based on the available survey demographic and income data. They find that individuals systematically underestimate their computed MTRs.[4] Romich and Weisner (2000) find that a high fraction of low-income households do not correctly perceive MTRs implied by the Earned Income Tax Credit (EITC) for hypothetical levels of income. In particular, the respondents' knowledge appears to be based on experience within their current income range, which they incorrectly extrapolate to other income ranges.[5]

Building on the idea of complexity, Liebman and Zeckhauser (2004) propose a simple hypothesis for how households interpret tax liability, or, equivalently, net income shocks. They suggest that households "schmedule," that is, approximate their true MTR by the average tax rate realized in the previous year, and provide some supportive evidence for this claim. They do not conceptually distinguish between predictable and unpredictable income innovations, as we do here. In fact, we will show in the next section that their hypothesis is a special case of the more general updating model that we develop.

A related, and rapidly growing, strand of literature focuses on the hypothesis that certain taxes, or certain ways of framing them, may be more salient in comparison with

---

[4]This interpretation is, however, sensitive to the assumption on the use of itemized deductions.

[5]For example, households who are in the phase-in portion of the EITC often assume that the amount of the credit increases linearly with the amount of labor income, even though the amount of the credit flattens out after a certain income threshold, and after another threshold it decreases.

other taxes or other ways of framing them. The empirical evidence generally suggests that the behavioral responses to taxes can be affected by issues of salience. For example, de Bartolome (1995) provides experimental evidence based on revealed choices that when the tax schedule is presented as a table mapping taxable income to the amount of tax entry by entry (as in the table accompanying the personal income tax form 1040), "there are at least as many individuals who use the average tax rate 'as if' it were the marginal tax rate, as individuals who use the true marginal tax rate."[6] Chetty et al. (2009), using both a field experiment and an observational study, find that consumer demand depends on whether a consumption tax is included in the posted price despite the fact that the final after-tax price is the same in either case.[7]

A number of laboratory experiment papers consider issues of salience. Blumkin et al. (2013) provide experimental evidence that an income tax induces a greater reduction in labor supply than does a theoretically equivalent consumption tax. They attribute this finding to the fact that direct taxes on income are more salient than indirect taxes on consumption. Feldman and Ruffle (2013) find that subjects in a laboratory setting who face final prices broken down into sales tax and pre-tax prices spend more than subjects who face tax inclusive prices. This finding is robust to learning and feedback. Abeler and Jäger (2013) test how complexity of the tax system in the lab impacts how subjects react to changes in economic incentives. They find that subjects in the complex tax treatment (as opposed to the simple tax treatment) underreact to changes in the tax system and, in fact, a large number do not react at all.

Misperceptions about the tax system that arise because of non-salient aspects of the

---

[6]However, given that as many as 85 percent of taxpayers nowadays rely either on a tax preparer or tax preparation software, the significance of tax schedule framing for taxpayer decisions potentially may affect only a relatively small and declining portion of taxpayers.

[7]Similar results have been obtained experimentally for private goods and services markets. For example, Hossain and Morgan (2006) find that a seller can raise a higher revenue in eBay auctions by cutting the reserve price and increasing the (less salient) shipping cost by the same amount. Choi et al. (2008) find that subjects pick higher fee index funds when allocating fictional investment despite the funds being based on the same index if the fee information is obfuscated by descriptions of past manager performances.

tax system have normative implications for social welfare. Chetty et al. (2009) develop a sufficient statistic approach for understanding the welfare implications of tax salience. Reck (2013) provides a generalization of their sufficient statistics approach.

# 2 Model

In this section, we formalize a model that describes how households interpret changes to their after-tax income, or equivalently, their realized tax liability. Suppose that a household faces a linear tax schedule in every period $t \in \{0, ..., T\}$ of its lifetime with the MTR given by $\tau_t$ and the demogrant (or intercept that is typically negative) given by $D_t$. Thus, in period $t$, a household with taxable income $y \geq 0$ has a tax liability determined by $L_t(y) = D_t + \tau_t y$. In practice, tax schedules are predominantly only piecewise linear, so the proposed linear schedule can be thought of as a local approximation of an otherwise more complicated tax scheme in a relevant range. The tax schedule varies across households because of differences in demographic characteristics such as the number of children and their ages, taxpayers' ages and disability status, as well as sources of income.

The tax schedule that households face can change over time for several reasons. First, a household may switch across different linear segments of a more complicated (and more realistic) piecewise linear tax schedule. Second, households may experience predictable changes to the tax schedule they face due to a variety of provisions. An example of a predictable tax liability change is that a household loses the Child Tax Credit (CTC) when a previously eligible child turns 17. Another example is that some tax cuts come with sunset provisions. Also, there could be tax consequences of planned actions, such as mortgage interest payments. These changes are, under a stable tax system, predictable many years in advance but not necessarily anticipated by taxpayers. Lastly, households may experience unpredictable changes to the tax schedule. Such changes could result from tax reforms or realizations of states of the world that have tax consequences, such as medical expenditures, disabilities, or the number and timing of children. In what follows, we focus on predictable changes in the tax schedule. Unpredictable changes are obviously realistic, and they can easily be incorporated into the analysis without qualitatively affecting the results.

We first identify two types of misperceptions that taxpayers may have about predictable changes to the tax system: *ex ante* and *ex post* misperceptions. In the case of *ex ante* misperceptions, taxpayers fail to anticipate a future change in the tax schedule that they face even though such a change is predictable. When experiencing *ex ante* misperceptions, households may fail to intertemporally optimize their behavior and thus exhibit "excess behavioral sensitivity" to predictable changes in the tax schedule.[8]

In the case of *ex post* misperceptions, taxpayers misinterpret a change in the tax schedule that they have already experienced. Consider a household that receives an unexpected tax refund. The household could plausibly reason that the refund came from a variety of sources, such as: (1) a lump-sum decrease in tax liability (e.g., the 2001 tax rebate); (2) a decrease in the MTR schedule (e.g., the Tax Reform Act of 1986); (3) or a timing shift in the receipt of after-tax income (e.g., the reduction in income tax withholding between 1991 and 1992).[9] With imperfect knowledge of the level and slope of the tax schedule, the unexpectedly high after-tax income realization could, in general, be partly interpreted in all three ways. In this case, taxpayers may respond to what they perceive as the source of the tax liability change.

---

[8]This argument is closely related to the permanent income hypothesis (PIH), in particular the finding that consumption tends to increase after a predictable income increase despite the absence of credit constraints.

[9]Of course, other interpretations over the source of this surprise are possible as well.

Formally, the parameters of the tax schedule that affect a household follow a process

$$
\begin{pmatrix} \tau_{t+1} \\ D_{t+1} \end{pmatrix} = \begin{pmatrix} \tau_t \\ D_t \end{pmatrix} + \begin{pmatrix} \phi_{\tau t+1} \\ \phi_{Dt+1} \end{pmatrix},
\tag{1}
$$

where $\phi_{t+1} \equiv (\phi_{\tau t+1}, \phi_{Dt+1})'$ is a vector of predictable changes in the parameters of the tax schedule between periods $t$ and $t+1$. However, the household may perceive these changes with an error, resulting in its expectation of the change $\phi_{t+1}^e$ diverging from the actual change $\phi_{t+1}$. In particular, from the point of the view of the household, $\phi_{t+1}^e -$ $\phi_{t+1}$ is a realization of $N(0, S_t)$, with realizations in different time periods assumed to be independent. Although this simplifying assumption rules out the possibility that a tax liability surprise is perceived as a pure shift in the timing of taxes, it simplifies the exposition and allows us to focus on the confusion between changes in the intercept and the slope of the tax schedule.

The matrix $S_t$ measures the household's ability to correctly perceive the predictable changes. For a perfectly informed household, $S_t = 0_{2\times2}$ and hence the predictable changes are in fact predicted without error. For a less than perfectly informed household, $S_t$ is a non-zero positive semi-definite matrix, meaning that $\phi_{t+1}^e$ is only a crude measure of the predictable change in the parameters of the tax schedule between periods $t$ and $t+1$. Although the normal distribution places a positive measure on the perceived MTR exceeding unity or falling below any arbitrary negative threshold, the stochastic specification in (1) may be thought of as a tractable approximation of beliefs over a bounded interval and we therefore overlook the problem of unboundedness in what follows.[10]

We also assume that the household does not necessarily have exact knowledge of the tax schedule when it first enters the labor force. In particular, prior beliefs over the MTR

---

[10]An alternative modeling strategy would be to assume mean reversion in the parameters of the tax schedule. This was done in a previous version of the paper and is available upon request. The exposition becomes more complicated with no effect on the qualitative results.

and intercept of the tax schedule at the end of period 0 are given by

$$\begin{pmatrix} \tau_0 \\ D_0 \end{pmatrix} \sim N\left[\mu_0, \Sigma_0\right], \tag{2}$$

where $\mu_0$ is the vector of the actual parameters facing the household. Again, the matrix $\Sigma_0$ determines the extent to which the household is aware of the details of the tax schedule when it first enters the labor force. For a fully informed household, $\Sigma_0 = 0_{2\times2}$, while for a less than fully informed household, $\Sigma_0$ is a non-zero positive semi-definite matrix.

At the end of period $t$, the household files its tax return for that period.[11] Conditional on pre-tax income $y_t$ in period $t$, the household observes its tax liability $L_t = D_t + \tau_t y_t$ which serves as a signal for $(\tau_t, D_t)$. The following proposition characterizes the evolution of beliefs about the parameters of future tax schedules based on past and current realizations of tax liability.

**Proposition 1** *Suppose that $S_t$ is positive definite in all time periods, or that three of its elements are zero and the remaining diagonal element is positive. Then beliefs about the parameters of the tax schedule in period $s \in \{t+1, .., T\}$ at the end of period $t$ are given by a normal distribution with mean*

$$E_t\left[(\tau_s, D_s)'\right] = E_t\left[(\tau_t, D_t)'\right] + \sum_{u=t+1}^{s} \phi_u^e$$

$$= \mu_0 + \sum_{u=1}^{t} \Gamma_u \left[L_u - E_{u-1}(L_u|y_u)\right] + \sum_{u=1}^{s} \phi_u^e \tag{3}$$

*and variance*

$$Var_t\left[(\tau_s, D_s)'\right] = \Sigma_t + \sum_{u=t+1}^{s} S_t, \tag{4}$$

---

[11]In reality, households file their tax returns in the early part of the year following the tax year in question. However, as long as such filing has the potential to affect the behavior in the year of filing, the exact timing of the filing is less important. We assume it happens at the end of period $t$ for a simplicity of exposition.

*where $\Sigma_u$ is defined recursively by*

$$\Sigma_u = \frac{\det(\Sigma_{u-1} + S_u)}{(y_u, 1)\,(\Sigma_{u-1} + S_u)\,(y_u, 1)'} \begin{bmatrix} 1 & -y_u \\ -y_u & y_u^2 \end{bmatrix}, \quad u = 1, ..., t, \tag{5}$$

*and*

$$\Gamma_u \equiv \frac{(\Sigma_{u-1} + S_u)\,(y_u, 1)'}{(y_u, 1)\,(\Sigma_{u-1} + S_u)\,(y_u, 1)'}, \quad u = 1, ..., t. \tag{6}$$

**Proof.** See the Appendix. ■

Intuitively, in each time period $t$, relative to the previous time period $t - 1$, the mean of beliefs over $(\tau_s, D_s)^T$ for $s > t$ is adjusted based on the realization of the tax liability surprise $L_t - E_{t-1}(L_t|y_t)$, with the slopes of the adjustment given by $\Gamma_t$. Note that the surprise is only due to unexpected changes in the tax parameters since any possible income change is conditioned out.[12] The analytical form of $\Sigma_t$ underlines the fact that at the end of period $t$, $\tau_t y_t + D_t = L_t$ is known with certainty, and, hence, $\Sigma_t(y_t, 1)' = 0$. Signs of the effects of the realized tax surprise in period $t$ on the expected value of the beliefs over the parameters of future tax schedules are given by the signs of the elements of $\Gamma_t$. Given the assumptions on $S_t$, $(y_t, 1)\,(\Sigma_{t-1} + S_t)\,(y_t, 1)'$ is positive, and hence the signs of the elements $\Gamma_t$ depend upon the signs of the elements of $(\Sigma_{t-1} + S_t)\,(y_t, 1)'$.

As previously discussed, one would expect that an unexpectedly high realization of tax liability would lead the household to revise its beliefs over both the MTR and the intercept upwards. However, this relationship does not necessarily hold. We show that a sufficient condition for this intuitively appealing prediction is that the covariance in the perceived

---

[12]If one assumes that the household is only confused about the MTR, but not about the intercept, then all of the elements of $S_t$ and $\Sigma_0$ except for the element $(1, 1)$ are equal to zero. In this case Proposition 1 implies that all of the elements of $\Sigma_{t-1}$ except for the element $(1, 1)$ are equal to zero, and hence $\Gamma_t = (1/y_t, 0)'$. As a result, any unexpected hike in the tax liability is reflected in an increase in the expectation of future MTRs by the magnitude of the surprise in the realized *average tax rate*. If coupled with the assumption that there is no intercept in the tax schedule at any time period, this case corresponds to the "schmeduling" hypothesis considered by Liebman and Zeckhauser (2004). When schmeduling, a household predicts its MTR for the current period to coincide with the average tax rate realized in the previous period.

noise of predictable changes in $\tau$ and $D$ is not too negative and that year-to-year taxable income changes are moderate.

The following proposition formalizes this observation.

**Proposition 2** *Suppose that*

$$-[S_t]_{12} < \min \left\{ y_t[S_t]_{11}, \frac{[S_t]_{22}}{y_t} \right\}. \tag{7}$$

*Then there exists an $\varepsilon_t > 0$ such that if $|\Delta y_t| < \varepsilon_t$, then $[\Gamma_t]_{11}, [\Gamma_t]_{21} > 0$. That is, an unexpected positive shock in the realized tax liability increases the mean of the belief about both $\tau_t$ and $D_t$.*

**Proof.** See the Appendix. ∎

The key to our model's sufficient condition rests in the magnitude of the covariance of perceived changes in the MTR and the intercept. This sufficient condition is clearly satisfied in the case when given an increase in tax liability, individuals believe that both have increased. For example, an increase in the MTR is coupled with a fall in the value of credits and deductions the household can take. Alternatively, a household may experience an increase in tax liability and yet believe that the intercept decreased (e.g., there are more tax credits available) but at the same time its MTR increased by enough to offset the decrease in the intercept. If so, $\tau$ and $D$ are perceived to be negatively correlated. This is plausible as tax reforms often involve changes that both reduce tax rates and broaden the tax base. If this covariance is negative enough, our sufficient condition will not be satisfied.

Of course, taxpayers' perceptions over changes to tax parameters are unobservable to us. To devise an empirically testable hypothesis from our model, we assume that rational and well-informed households do not change their perception of current and future tax schedule parameters upon experiencing tax schedule or segment changes. The argument is particularly appealing for tax parameter changes that are predictable well in advance.

13

Rational and well-informed households will respond to the actual source of the tax liability change. In contrast, boundedly rational or less well-informed households may misinterpret realized tax liability surprises and react as Proposition 2 predicts. That is, they change their perception of future tax schedule parameters in a way that does not accord with their actual changes.

We assume that the impact of perceived changes in the tax parameters on economic choices follows the standard predictions had the household actually experienced the perceived changes. Suppose that a household experiences an increase in their tax liability and then assumes that this change derives from an increase in the intercept, an increase in MTR, or some combination of the two. In the case of labor supply, this change in the demogrant will induce a positive income effect, whereas the change in MTR induces a negative substitution effect. The overall impact of this tax liability change on labor supply will depend on the weights that the household places on the change coming from the demogrant versus the MTR. This is an important observation because the natural experiment employed in our identification strategy presented in the next section constitutes a lump-sum change in tax liability.

Before moving to our empirical strategy, we note a few technical remarks about the model. First, we treat $S_t$ and $\Sigma_0$ as exogenous, but in reality households have control over the precision of their knowledge of the tax schedule and its changes. This would suggest introducing an explicit cost of information acquisition and modeling the two variance matrices as endogenous outcomes (Feige and Pearce, 1976; Buiter, 1980; Sims, 2003; Reis, 2006; Demery and Duck, 2007). On a different note, the "size" of $S_t$ may be a function of income variation as well as information costs. For example, if household taxable income fluctuates in a relatively narrow range from one year to another, switches among different segments of the tax schedule are not so frequent and, hence, $S_t$ may be "small". On the other hand, $S_t$ may be substantially "larger" if the household experiences large year-to-year taxable income variation. Details of taxable income history may matter as well in that the household may have more precise beliefs and information about segments of the tax schedule experienced previously. Although these extensions are plausible and worth future exploration, the purpose of the current model is to provide a simple, analytical illustration of the mechanics of updating based on realized tax liability, so we proceed with exogenous $S_t$ and $\Sigma_0$. This can be understood as a reduced-form version of a more complete model with conscious as well as accidental information acquisition. Yet another potential modeling extension it to allow $\phi_s^e$ for $s > t$ to be updated in period $t$ based on the most recent available information. Incorporating this addition would not affect the central message of the model and we therefore omit it for simplicity.

# 3 Identification Strategy and Empirical Implementation

To test how taxpayers interpret predictable changes in their tax liability, we identify a source of predictable, lump-sum variation in after-tax income. This variation comes from an age-based discontinuity generated by the eligibility rules for the Child Tax Credit (CTC). The CTC was introduced in 1998 and provides a non-refundable credit for an eligible child below 17 years of age as of December 31 of the tax year.[13] At the same time, the Additional Child Tax Credit (ACTC) was introduced. This credit provides for limited refundability of the non-refundable part of the CTC for families with three or more qualifying children.[14]

Initially, the CTC amount was $400 per eligible child. The CTC was increased to $500

---

[13]There are several provisions in the tax code that make the tax schedule a function of whether a dependent child did or did not reach a certain age in a given tax year. One such provision is the loss in the eligibility for the personal exemption and the Earned Income Tax Credit for a dependent child who turns 19 (or 24, if a full time student). This provision has been exploited by Looney and Singhal (2006) and Dokko (2007) in order to estimate the effect of marginal tax rates on labor supply.

[14]These families could claim the non-refundable part of the CTC up to the amount of employee contributed social security and medicare taxes less any earned income tax credit they received.

for the 1999 and 2000 tax years, $600 for the 2001 and 2002 tax years, and $1,000 for the 2003 tax year, where it currently stands. In addition, beginning in 2001, the ACTC was expanded to allow *any* family to claim the non-refundable part of the CTC up to one tenth of the excess of their earned income over $10,000.[15] The CTC has historically been phased out with adjusted gross income above $110,000 for married couples filing a joint tax return[16] at the rate of 5 percent.[17]

Three features of the CTC make it a good natural experiment for our analysis. First, to be eligible for the credit, the dependent child must not have reached 17 years of age by December 31 of the tax year in question. Because the timing of a child's 17th birthday is perfectly predictable, so is the implied timing of the net income loss. Second, due to the ACTC, virtually any household with up to two dependents and labor income between $30,000 and $110,000 can take advantage of the full amount of the CTC within the time period we consider (2001-2008). As a result, the loss of the CTC constitutes a pure lump-sum change in both tax liability and after-tax income. Third, it is difficult to plan the timing of birth for a particular quarter, month, or day. Thus, among families whose children turn 17 just before the end of year $t$ or at the very beginning of year $t+1$, eligibility for the CTC is virtually exogenous.[18] Put together, losing the CTC generates an exogenous, predictable and lump-sum variation in net income.

To identify the effect of this variation in a household's tax liability on household labor supply, we compare the growth rate of household labor income between years $t$ and $t+1$

---

[15]The $10,000 threshold has been indexed to inflation over time. In addition, starting in 2004, the ACTC limit was increased to 15 percent of earned income in excess of the threshold. Families with three or more eligible children could still claim the non-refundable part of the CTC up to the amount of employee contributed social security and medicare taxes less any earned income tax credit they received if this limit turned out to be higher.

[16]The thresholds are $75,000 and $55,000 for single/head of household taxpayers and married taxpayers filing separately, respectively. None of these thresholds are indexed for inflation.

[17]That is, a household loses $0.05 of the credit for every extra dollar of adjusted gross income above the threshold.

[18]In section 5, we discuss evidence why this may not be the case and test the robustness of our results to the potential endogeneity in the timing of birth.

16

for households whose child turns 17 at the end of year $t$ (the treated group) to households whose child turns 17 at the beginning of year $t + 1$ (the control group).[19] We do this by estimating the following equation by OLS:

$$\Delta \ln Y_{it+1} = \beta_0 + \beta_1 T_{it} + \sum_{c=1}^{8} \alpha_c \mathtt{I}(Cohort = c) + \pi' X_{it+1} + u_{it+1} \qquad (8)$$

The dependent variable is the growth rate in household labor income between years $t$ and $t+1$.[20] In this equation, $T$ is an indicator for a household being in the treatment group, i.e., a household that has at least one child who turns 17 in December of year $t$.[21] As we will describe in the next section, we utilize eight {December $t$, January $t+1$} pairs, or "cohorts". Thus, we include cohort indicators, $\mathtt{I}(Cohort = c)$, to ensure that the correct treatment and control households are compared. The vector $X_{it+1}$ contains household demographic characteristics in year $t + 1$.

The null hypothesis is that households *ex post* understand the tax schedule that they face. There are two cases when this might occur. The first case is when households are fully rational and fully informed. In this case, households anticipate the tax schedule change *ex ante*, so there should be no resulting income or substitution effect on household labor supply because the tax liability change is lump-sum and predictable. In the second case, households are *ex ante* confused. That is, households are surprised by the increase in tax liability, but *ex post* understand that the tax liability change was due to the loss of the credit. In this case, there is a non-negative income effect on household labor supply (assuming that leisure is a normal good). In either case, an *ex post* understanding of the tax

---

[19] While the credit itself is lost in year $t$, tax liability is not realized until year $t + 1$.

[20] We focus on labor income as a proxy for labor supply for two reasons. First, labor income is a summary measure of labor supply that includes responses on the extensive and intensive margins, work effort, and job search effort. Second, there is no information on hours of labor supply in the tax return data that we use for our analysis.

[21] Some households may have more than one child who turns 17 in the relevant time window. Roughly 1.1% of our observations represent multiple births. Although this leads to a loss of multiple credits, we do not differentiate between single and multiple births in the analysis.

liability change implies that, combined with a possible tightening of liquidity constraints, there is a non-negative impact on household labor income in the subsequent year ($\beta_1 \geq 0$).

The alternative hypothesis is that households experience both *ex ante* and *ex post* misperceptions.[22] In this case, households both fail to anticipate the loss of the credit and misinterpret the change in tax liability as (at least partially) reflecting a change in their MTR. As under the null hypothesis, there is a non-negative income effect. Now, however, there may also be a negative substitution effect if households interpret the unexpected increase in tax liability as an increase in the MTR. As a result, the net effect on household labor supply in the subsequent year is ambiguous. If the income effect dominates, then $\beta_1 \geq 0$. Thus, a finding of $\beta_1 \geq 0$ will not allow us to distinguish between the null and alternative hypotheses. However, if $\beta_1 < 0$, it must be the case that households are *ex ante* and *ex post* confused, and that the substitution effect dominates the income effect.

# 4 Data

To implement our identification strategy, we construct a data set from the universe of U.S. federal tax filings.[23] We begin by identifying individuals who turn 17 between December 2001 and January 2009 using date of birth information from social security records.[24] For our main analysis, we restrict attention to those individuals with birthdays in either January or December.[25] We match these individuals to the parents who claim him as a dependent on their tax return in the year that he turns 17. We include only

---

[22]We do not consider the seemingly odd case where a household would correctly anticipate the source of a tax liability change *ex ante*, and then be confused by the source of the change after the fact.

[23]These data are housed at the IRS's Compliance Data Warehouse (CDW), which contains transcribed data from all individual tax returns and information returns that are filed between 1999 and 2010, along with social security administrative data.

[24]These are individuals born between December 1984 and January 1992. In principle, we could have obtained data for those born in 1982 and 1983 for our analysis. We identified individuals born in these years from social security data. However, there appears to be an error in the file identifying dependents for years 1999 and 2000, the years in which these individuals turn 17.

[25]We identify between 772,000 and 791,000 individuals born in either January or December of each year, split fairly equally between birth months.

those individuals who are claimed as a dependent in this year, excluding individuals who file their own tax return as a primary filer, and those claimed as a spouse in the year that he/she turns 17. We restrict attention to parents who are married couples who file a joint tax return.[26] These households form the basis of our sample.

We construct pair-wise cohorts of treated and control groups. For each cohort, the treated group consists of households that have at least one child who turns 17 in December of year $t$ and the control group consists of households that have at least one child who turns 17 in January of $t+1$. For example, the first cohort contains individuals born in either December 1984 or January 1985, i.e., those who turn 17 in either December 2001 or January 2002. We have eight cohorts that we include in our main analysis, with years $t$ between 2001 and 2008.

We collect income variables for the relevant $t$ and $t+1$ tax years. We also collect demographic information for the vector $X$ in equation (8), which contains the number of children, age and age squared of the primary filer, and state fixed effects. For each household in our sample, we compute marginal tax rates in year $t$ using NBER's TAXSIM calculator (Feenberg and Coutts, 1993). In addition, we compute the hypothetical marginal tax rates that a household would face after losing a dependent that is eligible for the CTC, holding income constant.

To implement our identification strategy, we require at least two consecutive years of data for each household in the sample. We apply several other sample restrictions to our data. First, households must be married filing jointly in both years considered. Second, we drop households who claim an age exemption for either the primary or secondary filer because we do not want to confound our results by retirement decisions. We also exclude households where the primary filer is younger than 33 years of age (which would put the primary filer at around 16 years of age at the time of birth of the child). Third, we only use

---

[26]In general, based on IRS statistics, over 95% of married households file jointly.

data on households who have adjusted gross income in the range of $30,000 and $90,000 in year $t-1$. This restriction is made to minimize falling into the phase-in and the phase-out ranges of the credit in years $t$ and $t+1$, in which the loss of the CTC potentially does impact MTRs. We restrict the sample based on income in the year prior to the base year so that the transitory component of income is plausibly exogenous to those in years that we consider for our analysis. We also exclude households whose marginal tax rates changes when we hypothetically remove a CTC-eligible dependent from the household.

Our final estimation sample includes 1,396,785 observations. Table 1 presents summary statistics of the limited demographic characteristics that tax return data provide as well as income data for the treatment and control groups. As the Table shows, our treatment and control groups look similar on all observable dimensions. The average age of the tax filer and the total number of dependent children (that includes those under the age of 24 if enrolled in school, otherwise under the age of 19) are very similar. Income related variables in the base year, such as adjusted gross income and the applicable marginal tax rate faced on taxable income also look similar providing some confidence that our division based on December/January birth is fairly random. Because our sample size is so large, a standard t-test on equality of means for each of the variables is generally rejected at the 5% level except for adjusted gross income.[27] In all subsequent analyses, we control for the limited demographic information that we have.

# 5    Results

## 5.1    Main Result

Table 2 reports our baseline results. We estimate equation (8) by cohort (columns (1) - (8)) and then pooling all cohorts together (columns (9) and (10)). Standard errors are

---

[27]Similar statistical differences were found in LaLumia et al. (2012).

robust to heteroskedasticity.[28] In each specification, we find that having at least one child turn 17 in December of year $t$ as compared to January of year $t+1$ has a negative impact on the growth rate in household labor income. These findings contradict the null hypothesis and support the alternative hypothesis, i.e., the presence of a substitution effect driven by an *ex post* misperception of the surprise in net after-tax income.[29]

The impact of losing the CTC on the growth rate of labor income ranges from -0.003 (in 2004) to -0.013 (in 2008) and are generally statistically significant at the one percent level. The exceptions are in 2004 and 2005, where the estimated coefficients are significant at the ten and five percent level, respectively. When we pool the data and include cohort fixed effects, we obtain an estimate of -0.006. Taking this last estimate as our baseline, we conclude that households whose children are born in the last month of year $t$ and turn 17 experience roughly 0.6 percentage points less labor income growth (p-value $< 0.001$) than households whose children are born in the first month of year $t+1$ and turn 17.

In column (10), we interact the treatment dummy with three indicators of base-year income (income in year $t-1$): $30 - 50K, $50-70K, and $70-90K and present the treatment effect for each of these interactions. The treatment effect is strongest for the lowest income category at -0.013 and this effect decreases with income. The middle income category shows a treatment effect of -0.005 while the highest income category shows no treatment effect. Because the loss of the credit is a fixed amount per child, the effect as a percentage of income is decreasing in income and, as we would expect, has a less noticeable impact. This heterogeneity in responses may also reflect that higher income households have a better understanding of the CTC eligibility rules.

Taking the results from columns (9) and (10), we next interpret them within an elasticity

---

[28]Standard errors are also clustered at the household level in the final two columns to take into account that some households may appear in multiple cohorts once pooling the data.

[29]Some of this effect may reflect a shift of labor supply to an untaxed informal sector rather than to leisure or household production. However, since we have no information on informal labor market earnings, we are not able to address this hypothesis.

framework. The time-weighted average of the CTC over the eight years of our data is equal to $900.[30] Households may attribute the $900 in increased tax liability to a change in the demogrant, a change in MTR, or some weighted average of both. Figure 1 plots the implied elasticity of household labor income with respect to the after-tax share that we derive from varying the fraction of the $900 that is perceived to be due to a MTR increase. To understand how we generate these implied elasticities, suppose for example that households attribute $450 of the $900 increase in tax liability to an increase in the MTR rather than to an increase in the demogrant. For the average household income in our sample of $61,282, this constitutes approximately a 0.734 percentage point increase in perceived MTR.[31] To compute the implied change in the after-tax rate based on this perceived change in MTR, we must make an assumption about the household's perceived MTR before the loss of the CTC. We assume that households perceive their MTR correctly on average at 16.8% (see Table 1), so the implied after-tax share increases from 83.2% to 82.47%. This constitutes approximately a 0.88 percent decrease in the after-tax share, implying the elasticity of labor income with respect to the after-tax share of 0.68.[32] A generally accepted range of labor supply elasticities with respect to the (net) wage rate reported in the literature is between 0.1 and 0.6 for the intensive margin.[33] Given that our implied elasticity estimates are slightly above the upper bound of this range if $450 of the tax increase is attributed to

---

[30]Recall that in 2001 and 2002, the CTC was $600, and from 2003 to 2008, it was $1000.

[31]This calculation is done within the affine tax schedule framework.

[32]Alternatively, households may believe that their MTR is actually equal to the average tax rate (ATR). On average, the ATR is equal to 0.0852 in our sample (after dropping negative ATRs). Analogous computations then reveal that the implied elasticity is 0.74.

[33]Measures of elasticity vary depending primarily on the sex, marital status and age restrictions of the sample. The elasticity for prime-age single workers ranges roughly between 0.1 and 0.3 (see, for example, Altonji (1986) and McClelland and Mok (2012) whereas the elasticity for married women tends to be higher. Using the PSID, Peterman (2013) estimates an elasticity of 0.2 for prime-age single males and 0.55 for married households. Ideally, we would like to break our results down by gender and separately consider the impact on males and females or even primary earners and secondary earners. Breaking down our household income by spouse is an extremely data and time intensive procedure. As such, we provide a household average rather than a breakdown by gender. In addition, we find that self employed households (those with at least 25% of their income from Schedule C) react more strongly to the loss of the CTC. This finding is intuitive as self employed individuals generally have more ability to change their earnings and the amount of earnings they report.

a higher perceived MTR, this suggests that households are likely to erroneously attribute more that half of their tax increase to an increase in the MTR.[34]

Next, we repeat the same exercise for households in the $30,000-$50,000 and the $50,000-$75,000 income ranges using the estimates from column 10. For the $30,000-$50,000 range, the implied elasticity estimate when $450 of the tax increase is attributed to an increase in the MTR and the initial perception of the MTR is given by the true average MTR is 1.09.[35] Comparing these estimates with the commonly identified range of elasticity estimates implies that nearly the entire credit loss is attributed to a higher perceived MTR.[36] For households in the income range of $50,000 to $70,000, we find that the implied baseline elasticity is 0.58.[37] Again, comparing these estimates with the commonly identified range of elasticity estimates implies that at least half of the tax increase is incorrectly attributed to a change in the MTR.[38] We omit complementary analysis for the upper income category as the estimated coefficient is essentially zero.

## 5.2 Robustness Tests

The validity of our identification strategy rests on the assumption that there is no spurious non-tax correlation between the outcome and the treatment variable. Despite the empirical design, the treatment variable may be correlated with unobserved changes in tastes for supplying labor. We examine potential violations of this assumption and their impact on our interpretation of the results. Both because our estimates across cohorts are

---

[34]If $600 of the tax increase is attributed to an increase in the MTR, the two elasticity estimates are 0.51 and 0.56, respectively. If the entire $900 of the tax increase is attributed to an increase in the MTR, the two elasticity estimates are 0.34 and 0.37, respectively.

[35]When we instead assume that the perceived MTR prior to the credit loss is equivalent to the ATR, the implied elasticity becomes 1.21.

[36]If $600 of the tax increase is attributed to an increase in the MTR, the two elasticity estimates using the MTR and ATR baselines are 0.82 and 0.91, respectively. If the entire $900 of the tax increase is attributed to an increase in the MTR, the two elasticity estimates are 0.54 and 0.60, respectively.

[37]The elasticity becomes 0.63 using the ATR baseline.

[38]If $600 of the tax increase is attributed to an increase in the MTR, the two elasticity estimates are 0.43 and 0.47, respectively. If the entire $900 of the tax increase is attributed to an increase in the MTR, the two elasticity estimates are 0.29 and 0.32, respectively.

very similar and because collecting additional observations is highly data intensive, our robustness tests that require additional data are done using two years of data, in particular 2006 and 2007. We selected these years both because the baseline results from the 2006 cohort fall in the middle of the range of estimates and because it falls well after the 2003 increase in the CTC to $1000 (and would be in favor of finding a potential effect in our placebos as compared to smaller credit values).

One concern is that there may be a direct effect of child aging on the growth rate of household labor income. Households in the treatment group have, on average, slightly older children than households in the control group. If the growth rate of household labor income depends on the age of their children, then our estimates of $\beta_1$ may confound the effect of losing the CTC with a direct effect of the child's age.[39] Given our baseline results, this concern is an issue only if parents *reduce* their labor income in response to child aging.

We first test whether there is a direct effect of child aging by comparing household labor income growth rates for households with children turning 17 in consecutive birth months within a tax year.[40] For example, we compare January ("treated") and February ("control") births within the same year. Households in the "treatment" and "control" groups have children with similar differences in age as our baseline specification, but there should be no difference in the tax consequences between the two groups. We run this placebo test 11 times, once for each set of consecutive months. The results are presented in Table 3. Only one of the differences between the "treated" and "control" households is statistically significant at the 5% level.[41]

---

[39]A first test to mitigate the concern is to narrow the window around December 31 in order to further minimize age differences between treatment and control. We re-estimated our baseline pooled sample restricting the cohort window to be for the last two weeks of December and the first two weeks of January. We find the baseline results are completely unaffected, the estimated coefficient is equal to -.006 and statistically significant at the one percent level.

[40]For this exercise, we collect data for all individuals who turned 17 in 2006 and therefore still receive the credit in 2006.

[41]In order to further investigate the one significant result on the March/April sample for the 2006 cohort, we repeated the March/April analysis on the 2007 and 2008 cohorts. Neither coefficient is statistically significant at conventional levels. The results are available from the authors upon request.

A related concern is that children in the treatment group may be one grade ahead of children in the control group if school entry cutoff dates occur at the end of a calendar year. To evaluate the relevance of this concern to our analysis, we perform two tests using information on state school enrollment rules to identify households where children in the treatment and control groups are likely to be in different academic school years. First, we note that children in our first cohort turned six years old in December of 1990 and January of 1991 and at that time, five states had a December 31 school entry cutoff date. For households in these states, this policy would lead to a one academic year difference between the treatment and control groups.[42] As the trend has been to move up school entry cutoff dates, applying the law from 1990 to our entire sample is the more conservative option. As shown in column (1) of Table 4, we find that when dropping these five states in addition to four additional states where the school entry cutoff date was determined by the local authority and not at the state level, the results are nearly identical to our baseline findings.[43]

As a second test for whether differences in academic school years affect household labor income growth rates, we make additional use of the 2006 monthly birth data. In particular, we purposely choose "treated" and "control" households to have children in different academic grades but to face the same tax situation. For example, we consider states with a September 1 school entry cutoff dates and compare households with a child born in July to a child born in October of the same year. Both turn 17 in year $t + 1$ but the child born in July finishes high school one year earlier than the child born in October (generally speaking). Overall, we consider the 32 states that have cutoff dates throughout August 31 - October 15 and choose households with children born, on average, about six weeks before and after the cutoffs. We consider those born before the cutoff as "treated" and those born

---

[42]Note that we observe the state in which the household lived in the respective year, which is not necessarily the state in which the child lived when he or she entered school a decade earlier. However, we speculate that it is the same state for most of the households.

[43]The states are CO, DE, HI, LA, MA, MD, NJ, RI, and WA.

after as "control." The results are presented in column (2) of Table 4. Households with at least one child born before the cutoff have roughly 0.4% higher labor income growth between years $t$ and $t+1$. This suggests that a child leaving home or entering college has a positive effect on household labor income. Thus, if the treated households in our baseline specification have children leaving the home sooner than the control households, such an effect would bias our results upwards and our main results are only strengthened.

If there is a direct effect of child aging on household labor supply, we should be able to detect some of this effect in earlier years. Using our sample of children who turn 17 in December 2006 or January 2007, we test whether there is a differential growth rate in household labor income when these same children turn 15 and when they turn 16. Results from these robustness tests appear in columns (3) and (4) of Table 4. The estimated placebo coefficients are numerically close to and statistically indistinguishable from zero at conventional levels of statistical significance.

As a final robustness test, we replicate our baseline estimate taking advantage of the fact that we know the exact birthdate of the children in our sample. In our main empirical strategy, households are assigned to the treatment and control group based solely on the basis of an observed continuous measure, i.e., days before of after January 1st. Therefore, we can construct a selection variable, $S_i$, defined as days prior to February 1st of year $t+1$ on which the relevant child for household $i$'s birthday falls. Observations where $S_i > 32$, i.e., when a child's birthday falls on December 31st, are treated with probability 1, while those for whom $S_i \leq 31$ are not. As an alternative method for estimating the treatment effect, we estimate a sharp regression discontinuity (RD) specification, given by:

$$\Delta \ln Y_{it+1} = \beta_0 + \beta_1 T_{it} + \gamma_1 S_i + \gamma_2 S_i^2 + \gamma_3 S_i^3 + \sum_{c=1}^{8} \alpha_c \mathrm{I}(Cohort = c) + \pi' X_{it+1} + u_{it+1}. \quad (9)$$

The results are presented in column (5) of Table 4. As seen, the results are virtually

26

identical to our baseline estimate.

Overall, these robustness tests show that the baseline estimates presented in Table 2 do not appear to be driven by a direct effect of child aging on household labor income nor spurious correlation due to the end of the tax year. Put together, these robustness tests document that a direct effect of child aging cannot account for the baseline estimates, which therefore appear to be driven by the loss of the CTC.[44]

# 6 Discussion

Our results relate to the tests of the permanent income hypothesis (PIH). Both applications share the prediction that predictable lump-sum changes in disposable income should not, barring credit constraints, have any effect on the behavior of the household. The basic difference between the PIH literature and our empirical application is that the former focuses on household consumption as the outcome variable, whereas we focus on household labor income, which proxies for labor supply.

The existing evidence on the PIH is mixed. Some studies support the PIH (Browning and Collado, 2001; Coulibaly and Li, 2006), while others find that consumption increases with positive predictable income shocks (Parker, 1999; Souleles, 1999, 2002; Stephens, 2003; Shapiro and Slemrod, 2003; Johnson et al., 2006). Hsieh (2003) puts forth a resolution to this puzzle: households may respond to relatively large anticipated income changes, but not to smaller anticipated changes. As evidence, Hsieh (2003) documents that Alaskan households do not increase their consumption when paid from the (oil revenue-based) Alaska

---

[44]In addition to the concerns that we address, Dickert-Conlin and Chandra (1999) argue that if a child is to be born around the turn of the year, parents may have a preference to speed up the birth on the margin so that they can claim tax benefits for the ending calendar year. The authors also find that such behavior is more prevalent among higher income households, raising another potential spurious correlation problem. However, this problem does not pose a concern for our interpretation of the results since it implies that we tend to underestimate $\beta_1$ in absolute value as more sophisticated taxpayers would be less subject to *ex ante* and *ex post* confusion, suggesting that the true coefficient is even more negative. Further, more recent analysis by LaLumia et al. (2012) using the universe of tax returns finds that such an effect is quite small.

Permanent Fund, but that the very same households do increase their consumption in response to an annual federal income tax refund. He notes that "...many tax and fiscal policy measures will probably have an effect on aggregate consumption as long as people find it difficult and costly to understand precisely how their incomes are affected by these policies." This reasoning suggests that whether a particular predictable change in net income is incorporated into consumption plans may depend on the *ex ante* salience of the change.

Our results suggest that a similar claim applies to the *ex post* interpretation of predictable net income changes. Indeed, if *ex ante* misperceptions of an income change are driven by information costs or bounded rationality, then there is no reason to expect perfect *ex post* understanding either. In the case of consumption, *ex post* misperceptions mean that a household has biased beliefs about the extent to which an income shock is temporary versus permanent, with implications for the optimal consumption plan. Even if the duration of the shock is known, a lack of knowledge about its source except that it comes from taxes may have implications for perception of net prices and hence decisions on margins such as labor supply, retirement saving, and charitable contributions.

Our study also relates to the literature on strategic price obfuscation. In these models, if consumers have misperceptions of their true marginal user price of goods, then designers of pricing schemes may strategically use this to their advantage.[45] Such an argument seemingly extends to any market with a monopoly provider, be it a public or a private good. In particular, a failure to deal with the complexity of a tax system may, apart from being an outcome of a political process, also be interpreted as a strategic choice by the government if taxpayers underestimate their MTR as a result.

---

[45]It may seem that such price obfuscation will not survive in competitive markets for private goods since competing firms will have an incentive to educate their competitors' customers via advertising. However, this is not necessarily the case. For example, Gabaix and Laibson (2006) show that in the presence of myopic consumers, firms will strategically shroud prices of add-on products such as printer cartridges in order to obfuscate the true cost of product usage. In addition, they show that in equilibrium there is a "debiasing curse" in that firms may not have incentives to educate their competitors' myopic customers because then they would not be able to win over their business once debiased. Elisson (2006) provides an in-depth review of various theoretical approaches to modeling how firms strategically obfuscate prices.

Several papers extend the notion of price obfuscation to taxes. Finkelstein (2009) argues that if a particular tax or levy is less salient, then the tax base is less elastic to it. This, in turn, implies that the optimal tax or tax rate is higher. To support her claim, she documents that freeway toll charges are higher in places that use electronic toll debiting compared to places that collect tolls in cash. Reflecting on the results of Blumkin et al. (2013) and Chetty et al. (2009), it may be advantageous to tax consumption rather than income and, if possible, to minimize the salience of consumption taxes by developing legal and social norms under which posted prices exclude the tax. Homonoff and Goldin (2013) find that lower income individuals are more attentive to register taxes on cigarettes than are higher income individuals (and both are equally responsive to posted commodity taxes). Therefore, the government can take advantage of the heterogeneity in attentiveness to reduce the regressivity of cigarette taxation by a revenue-neutral shift from posted to register taxes. Goldin (2013) shows that policymakers can employ tax intruments of varying salience to achieve the first-best welfare outcome even in the absence of a lump-sum tax.

# 7 Conclusion

Due to complexity of the income tax system, taxpayers may have difficulties recognizing their true marginal tax rate. As a result, they may turn to rules of thumb in approximating how much of an additional dollar of income is taken away in taxes. We present a formal model in which households have only a limited understanding of the tax schedule they face and update their estimate of the current year's marginal tax rate based on the previous year's unexpected innovation in the realized tax liability. This in general leads to *ex post* tax schedule misperceptions, particularly misperceptions about the MTR. Under the assumption that taxpayers react to perceived after-tax incentives as predicted by economic theory, we examine the validity of the misperception hypothesis by measuring taxpayer labor income responses to an exogenous, lump-sum and predictable variation in the tax liability due to losing eligibility for the Child Tax Credit when the child turns 17.

We find that households who lose the credit due to having their child turn 17 at the end of a calendar year have a lower growth rate of household labor income in the subsequent year compared to households that have their child turn 17 at the beginning of the following calendar year. This result is inconsistent with households being fully informed about the loss of the CTC. Instead, we argue that households are misinterpreting the increase in their tax bill as (at least partly) reflecting an increase in their MTR which leads to a reduction in labor supply due to the conventional substitution effect. This finding is robust to a variety of tests that include placebo effects at various other age and calendar cutoffs. We interpret this finding as evidence for the presence of the substitution effect on labor supply and evidence for imperfect *ex post* understanding of the CTC loss. In fact, our estimates suggest that more than half of the increased tax burden is perceived to be due to an increase in the MTR.

Taken at face value, our results suggest that tax policy changes that are not well-understood or predicted by the affected population, despite being predictable, may have unintended behavioral and welfare consequences. In particular, changes that affect the level but not the slope of the tax schedule may result in a substitution effect that is not intended, hence increasing or reducing the deadweight loss relative to the full information case. On the other hand, changes that mostly affect the marginal tax rate may be partly interpreted as changes in the level of the tax schedule, with analogous implications for the deadweight loss. The complexity of the tax system may therefore interact with tax changes to create departures from conventionally understood welfare effects. This reasoning suggests that whenever households are likely to overshoot, relative to reality, their beliefs about the marginal tax rate, providing more and better information may be beneficial. On the other hand, just the opposite is the case when households are likely to undershoot.

The simple theoretical model presented in this paper leaves several open areas for future research. First, if households face a tax schedule about which they have imperfect knowledge, they may in principle experiment in order to obtain more information. That is, there may be a feedback effect from the choice of labor income to the process of belief evolution over time. Second, it is likely that the error variance in predicting changes in the tax schedule is determined endogenously by conscious information-gathering actions. For example, this variance can be reduced by investing time to learn about the tax code or hiring a tax advisor. Likewise, more empirical work based on alternative sources of tax schedule variation is needed as well in order to refine our understanding of when and under what circumstances taxpayers are likely to experience particular misperceptions of their tax schedule.

# References

**Abeler, Johannes and Simon Jäger**, "Complex Tax Incentives," *CESifo Working Paper 4231*, 2013.

**Altonji, Joseph**, "Intertemporal Substitution in Labor Supply: Evidence from Micro Data," *The Journal of Political Economy*, 1986, *93* (3), 176–215.

**Auten, Gerald and Robert Carroll**, "The Effect of Income Taxes on Household Income," *Review of Economics and Statistics*, 1999, *81* (4), 681–693.

**Blumkin, Tomer, Yosi Ganun, and Bradley J. Ruffle**, "Are Income and Consumption Taxes Ever Really Equivalent? Evidence from a Real-Effort Experiment," *European Economic Review,*, 2013, *56* (6), 1200–19.

**Brown, C. V.**, "Misconceptions About Income Tax and Incentives," *Scottish Journal of Political Economy*, 1968, *15* (1), 1–21.

**Browning, M. Dolores and Martin Collado**, "The Response of Expenditures to Anticipated Income Changes: Panel Data Estimates," *American Economic Review*, 2001, *91* (3), 681–692.

**Buiter, W. H.**, "Macroeconomics of Pangloss - Critical Survey of the New Classical Macroeconomics," *Economic Journal*, 1980, *90* (357), 34–50.

**Chetty, Raj, Adam Looney, and Kory Kroft**, "Salience and Taxation: Theory and Evidence," *American Economic Review*, 2009, *99*, 1145–77.

_ , **John Friedman, and Emmanuel Saez**, "Using Differences in Knowledge Across Neighborhoods to Uncover the Impacts of EITC on Earnings," *American Economic Review*, forthcoming.

**Choi, James, David Laibson, and Bridgette Madrian**, "Why Does the Law of One Price Fail? An Experiment on Index Mutual Funds," Yale ICF Working Paper No. 08-14 April 2008.

**Coulibaly, Brahima and Geng. Li**, "Do Homeowners Increase Consumption After the Last Mortgage Payment? An Alternative Test of the Permanent Income Hypothesis," *Review of Economics and Statistics*, 2006, *88* (1), 10–19.

**de Bartolome, Charles**, "Which Tax Rate Do People Use - Average or Marginal," *Journal of Public Economics*, 1995, *56* (1), 79–96.

**DeGroot, Morris**, *Optimal Statistical Decisions*, McGraw-Hill, 1970.

**Demery, David and Nigel Duck**, "The Theory of Rational Expectations and the Interpretation of Macroeconomic Data," *Journal of Macroeconomics*, 2007, *29* (1), 1–18.

**Dickert-Conlin, S. and A. Chandra**, "Taxes and the Timing of Births," *Journal of Political Economy*, 1999, *107* (1), 161–77.

**Dokko, Jane**, "The Effect of Taxation on Lifecycle Labor Supply: Results from a Quasi-Experiment," FED Working Paper No. 2008-24 September 2007.

**Eissa, Nada**, "Taxation and Labor Supply of Married Women: The Tax Reform Act of 1986 as a Natural Experiment," NBER Working Paper 5023, February 1995.

_ **and Jeffrey B. Liebman**, "Labor Supply Response to the Earned Income Tax Credit," *Quarterly Journal of Economics*, 1996, *111* (2), 605–637.

**Elisson, Glenn**, "Bounded Rationality in Industrial Organization," in R. Blundell, W. Newey, and T. Persson, eds., *Advances in Economics and Econometrics: Theory and Applications, Ninth World Congress*, Vol. 2, Cambridge University Press, 2006, pp. 142–174.

**Feenberg, Dan and Elizabeth Coutts**, "An Introduction to the Taxsim Model," *Journal of Policy Analysis and Management*, 1993, *12* (1), 189–194.

**Feige, Edgar and Douglas Pearce**, "Economically Rational Expectations - Are Innovations in Rate of Inflation Independent of Innovations in Measures of Monetary and Fiscal Policy?," *Journal of Political Economy*, 1976, *84* (3), 499–522.

**Feldman, Naomi and Bradley Ruffle**, "The Impact of Tax Exclusive and Inclusive Prices on Demand," *Working Paper*, 2013.

**Feldstein, Martin**, "The Effect of Marginal Tax Rates on Taxable Income: A Panel Study of the 1986 Tax Reform Act," *Journal of Political Economy*, 1995, *103* (3), 551–572.

**Finkelstein, Amy**, "E-ZTax: Tax Salience and Tax Rates," *Quarterly Journal of Economics*, 2009, *124* (3).

**Fujii, E. T. and C. B. Hawley**, "On the Accuracy of Tax Perceptions," *Review of Economics and Statistics*, 1988, *70* (2), 344–347.

**Gabaix, Xavier and David Laibson**, "Shrouded Attributes, Consumer Myopia, and Information Suppression in Competitive Markets," *Quarterly Journal of Economics*, 2006, *121* (2), 505–540.

**Goldin, Jacob**, "Optimal Tax Salience," Working Paper, 2013.

**Goolsbee, Austan**, "What Happens When You Tax the Rich? Evidence from Executive Compensation," *Journal of Political Economy*, 2000, *108* (2), 352–378.

**Gruber, Jonathan and Emmanuel Saez**, "The Elasticity of Taxable Income: Evidence and Implications," *Journal of Public Economics*, 2002, *84* (1), 1–32.

**Homonoff, Tatiana and Jacob Goldin**, "Smoke Gets in Your Eyes: Cigarette Tax Salience and Regressivity," *American Economic Journal: Economic Policy,*, 2013, *5* (1), 302–36.

**Hossain, Tanjim and John Morgan**, "...Plus Shipping and Handling: Revenue (Non) Equivalence in Field Experiments on eBay," *B.E. Journals in Economic Analysis and Policy: Advances in Economic Analysis and Policy*, 2006, *6* (2), 1–27.

**Hsieh, Chang-Tai**, "Do Consumers React to Anticipated Income Changes? Evidence from the Alaska Permanent Fund," *American Economic Review*, 2003, *93* (1), 397–405.

**Johnson, David, Jonathan Parker, and Nicholas Souleles**, "Household Expenditure and the Income Tax Rebates of 2001," *American Economic Review*, 2006, *96* (5), 1589–1610.

**Kopczuk, Wojciech**, "The Optimal Elasticity of Taxable Income," *Journal of Public Economics*, 2005, *84* (1), 91–112.

**LaLumia, Sara, James Sallee, and Nicholas Turner**, "New Evidence on Taxes and the Timing of Birth," Manuscript 2012.

**Liebman, Jeffrey B. and Richard J. Zeckhauser**, "Schmeduling," Manuscript, Harvard, October 2004.

**Looney, Adam and Monica Singhal**, "The Effect of Anticipated Tax Changes on Intertemporal Labor Supply and the Realization of Taxable Income," FED Working Paper No. 2005-44 September 2006.

**McClelland, Robert and Shannon Mok**, "A Review of Recent Research on Labor Supply Elasticities," CBO Working Paper No. 2012-12 October 2012.

**Parker, Jonathan A.**, "The Reaction of Household Consumption to Predictable Changes in Social Security Taxes," *American Economic Review*, 1999, *89* (4), 959–973.

**Peterman, William**, "Reconciling Micro and Macro Estimates of the Frisch Labor Supply Elasticity," *Working Paper*, 2013.

**Poterba, James M. and Andrew Samwick**, "Taxation and Household Portfolio Composition: US Evidence from the 1980s and 1990s," *Journal of Public Economics*, 2003, *87* (1), 5–38.

**Reck, Daniel**, "Taxes and Mistakes: What's in a Sufficient Statistic?," Manuscript 2013.

**Reis, Ricardo**, "Inattentive Consumers," *Journal of Monetary Economics*, 2006, *53* (8), 1491–1530.

**Romich, Jennifer and Thomas Weisner**, "How Families View and Use the EITC: Advance Payment versus Lump Sum Delivery," *National Tax Journal*, 2000, *53* (4), 1245–1265.

**Saez, Emmanuel**, "Reported Incomes and Marginal Tax Rates, 1960-2000: Evidence and Policy Implications," in James M. Poterba, ed., *Tax Policy and the Economy*, Vol. 18, The MIT Press, 2004, pp. 117–173.

**Shapiro, Mathew and Joel Slemrod**, "Consumer Response to Tax Rebates," *American Economic Review*, 2003, *93* (1), 381–396.

**Sims, Christopher**, "Implications of Rational Inattention," *Journal of Monetary Economics*, 2003, *50* (3), 665–690.

**Souleles, Nicholas S.**, "The Response of Household Consumption to Income Tax Refunds," *American Economic Review*, 1999, *89* (4), 947–958.

_ , "Consumer Response to the Reagan Tax Cuts," *Journal of Public Economics*, 2002, *85* (1), 99–120.

**Stephens, Melvin**, ""3rd of the Month": Do Social Security Recipients Smooth Consumption Between Checks?," *American Economic Review*, 2003, *93* (1), 406–422.

**Turner, Nicholas**, "Why Don't Taxpayers Maximize their Tax-Based Student Aid? Salience and Inertia in Program Selection," *The B.E. Journal of Economic Analysis and Policy*, 2011, *11* (64), 977–1000.

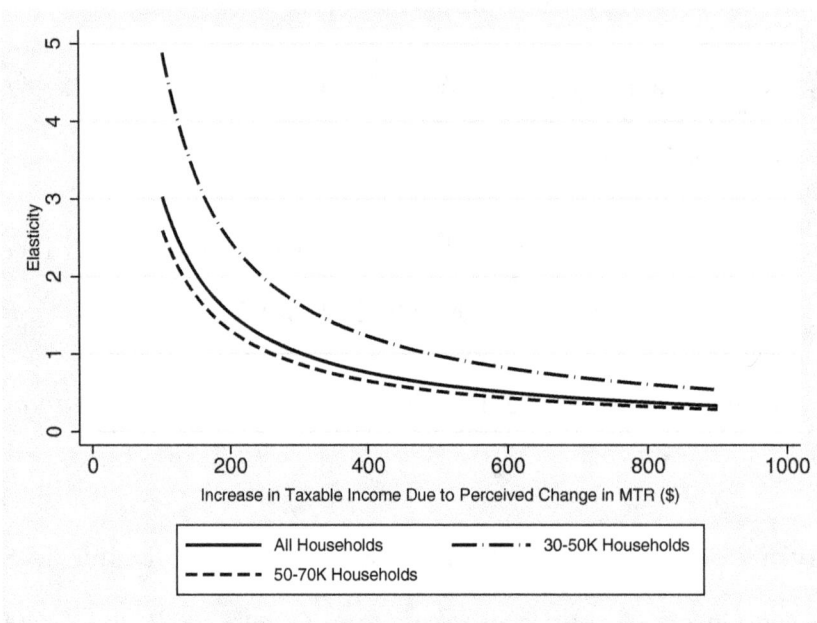

Figure 1: Labor Income Elasticity

1. The figure presents the labor income elasticities that result from varying the change in after tax income due to the loss of the CTC that is perceived to be due to a change in the marginal tax rate.

2. The base MTR is equal to the average MTR in the data (see Table 1).

Table 1: Demographic Summary Statistics

|  | Control | | Treatment | |
|  | Mean | Std. Dev. | Mean | Std. Dev. |
| --- | --- | --- | --- | --- |
| Age of the primary filer | 46.72 | 5.73 | 46.80 | 5.75 |
| Number of children | 2.25 | 1.09 | 2.19 | 1.11 |
| MTR on next dollar of wage earnings | 16.71 | 7.86 | 16.84 | 7.88 |
| Adjusted gross income in base year | 59545.65 | 16358.41 | 59526.98 | 16380.08 |
| | | | | |
| *Obs.* | 683,322 | | 713,463 | |

*Source:* Authors' calculations using individual tax return data.

Table 2: The Effect of Losing CTC Eligibility on household labor Income

| | (1) | (2) | (3) | (4) | (5) | (6) | (7) | (8) | (9) | (10) |
|---|---|---|---|---|---|---|---|---|---|---|
| YEAR | 2001 | 2002 | 2003 | 2004 | 2005 | 2006 | 2007 | 2008 | 2001-2008 | 2001-2008 |
| T | -0.007*** | -0.006*** | -0.006*** | -0.003* | -0.004** | -0.005*** | -0.005*** | -0.013*** | -0.006*** | |
| | (0.002) | (0.002) | (0.002) | (0.002) | (0.002) | (0.002) | (0.002) | (0.002) | (0.001) | |
| T30-50 | | | | | | | | | | -0.013*** |
| | | | | | | | | | | (0.001) |
| T50-70 | | | | | | | | | | -0.005*** |
| | | | | | | | | | | (0.001) |
| T70-90 | | | | | | | | | | 0.000 |
| | | | | | | | | | | (0.000) |
| Constant | -0.448*** | -0.481*** | -0.342*** | -0.267*** | -0.248*** | -0.373*** | -0.427*** | -0.477*** | -0.387*** | -0.389*** |
| | (0.052) | (0.055) | (0.054) | (0.051) | (0.053) | (0.054) | (0.054) | (0.059) | (0.019) | (0.019) |
| Observations | 185,673 | 182,216 | 178,066 | 181,022 | 175,380 | 172,907 | 164,682 | 156,762 | 1,396,708 | 1,396,708 |
| R-squared | 0.003 | 0.002 | 0.002 | 0.002 | 0.002 | 0.003 | 0.004 | 0.005 | 0.007 | 0.007 |

*Notes:*

1. The dependent variable is $\Delta log(wage income)_{t+1}$. Control variables (estimates not displayed) are age and age squared of the tax filer, total number of dependents in the household and its squared term, state and year (columns 9 and 10 only) fixed effects.

2. Heteroskedasticity-robust standard errors in parentheses and additionally clustered at household level in columns 9 and 10.

3. Significant at: *** 1 percent, ** 5 percent, * 10 percent.

38

Table 3: The Effect of Losing CTC Eligibility on household labor Income

| | (1) JAN/FEB | (2) FEB/MAR | (3) MAR/APR | (4) APR/MAY | (5) MAY/JUN | (6) JUN/JUL | (7) JUL/AUG | (8) AUG/SEP | (9) SEP/OCT | (10) OCT/NOV | (11) NOV/DEC |
|---|---|---|---|---|---|---|---|---|---|---|---|
| T | 0.001 | 0.000 | -0.004** | 0.002 | -0.001 | -0.000 | 0.000 | 0.002 | 0.002 | -0.001 | -0.001 |
| | (0.002) | (0.002) | (0.002) | (0.002) | (0.002) | (0.002) | (0.002) | (0.002) | (0.002) | (0.002) | (0.002) |
| Constant | -0.291*** | -0.324*** | -0.347*** | -0.348*** | -0.369*** | -0.338*** | -0.249*** | -0.242*** | -0.276*** | -0.263*** | -0.325*** |
| | (0.058) | (0.056) | (0.052) | (0.053) | (0.054) | (0.050) | (0.048) | (0.050) | (0.052) | (0.052) | (0.052) |
| Observations | 125,836 | 130,862 | 135,076 | 135,208 | 139,619 | 143,426 | 149,303 | 150,645 | 147,313 | 140,465 | 137,651 |
| R-squared | 0.0038 | 0.004 | 0.003 | 0.003 | 0.003 | 0.003 | 0.003 | 0.003 | 0.003 | 0.003 | 0.003 |

*Notes:*

1. The dependent variable is equal to $\Delta log(wage income)_{t+1}$. Control variables (estimates not displayed) are age and age squared of the tax filer, total number of dependents in the household and its squared term, state and year (columns 9 and 10 only) fixed effects.

2. The estimation sample consists of all households who have at least one child who turns 17 in 2006-2007.

3. Heteroskedasticity-robust standard errors in parentheses.

4. Significant at: *** 1 percent, ** 5 percent, * 10 percent.

Table 4: Robustness Tests

| | No Dec. Cutoff | Dif. Academic Year | Turning 15 | Turning 16 | RD |
|---|---|---|---|---|---|
| | (1) | (2) | (3) | (4) | (5) |
| T | -0.006*** | 0.004** | 0.000 | -0.002 | -0.006*** |
| | (0.001) | (0.002) | (0.002) | (0.002) | (.002) |
| Constant | -0.393*** | -0.235*** | -0.208*** | -0.278*** | -0.386*** |
| | (0.021) | (.063) | (0.047) | (0.049) | (0.019) |
| Obs | 1,225,174 | 80958 | 174,847 | 170,887 | 1,396,708 |
| R-squared | 0.007 | 0.003 | 0.002 | 0.002 | 0.007 |

*Notes:*

1. Dependent variable equal to $\Delta log(wageincome)_{t+1}$. Control variables (estimates not displayed) are age and age squared of the tax filer, total number of dependents in the household and its squared term, and state fixed effects.

2. Heteroskedasticity-robust standard errors in parentheses and clustered at the household level in columns 1 and 5. Year fixed effects are included in columns 1 and 5.

3. Column 1: full baseline sample; column 2: sample consists of households whose children turn 17 in 2007 (the control group of the 2006 cohort) and live in states with school entry cutoff dates ranging between August 31 - October 15; Columns 3 and 4: 2006 cohort in earlier years. Column 5 estimates Equation 9 on the full pooled sample.

4. Significant at: *** 1 percent, ** 5 percent, * 10 percent.

# A  Mathematical Appendix

**Proof of Proposition 1.** Choose an arbitrary time period $u \in \{0, ..., T\}$. Suppose that, based on the initial beliefs in period 0 and all the signals accumulated up until the end of period $u - 1$, the household beliefs about $(\tau_{u-1}, D_{u-1})$ are given by $N(\mu_{u-1}, \Sigma_{u-1})$. Due to expected changes in the tax schedule, the beliefs about $(\tau_u, D_u)$ at the beginning of period $u$ are given by $N(\mu_{u-1} + \phi_u^e, \Sigma_{u-1} + S_u)$. Then the joint distribution of $\tau_u$, $D_u$, and $T_u$ is given by

$$\begin{pmatrix} \tau_u \\ D_u \\ T_u \end{pmatrix} \sim N \left\{ \begin{pmatrix} \mu_{u-1} + \phi_u^e \\ (y_u, 1)(\mu_{u-1} + \phi_u^e) \end{pmatrix}, \begin{bmatrix} \Sigma_{u-1} + S_u & (\Sigma_{u-1} + S_i)(y_u, 1)^T \\ (y_{iu}, 1)(\Sigma_{iu-1} + S_i) & (y_u, 1)(\Sigma_{u-1} + S_u)(y_u, 1)^T \end{bmatrix} \right\}. \tag{10}$$

Based on observing the realization of $T_u$, the posterior belief about $(\tau_u, D_u)$ is then given by (DeGroot, 1970)

$$\begin{pmatrix} \tau_u \\ D_u \end{pmatrix} \sim N \left\{ \mu_{u-1} + \phi_u^e + \Gamma_u \left[ T_u - E_{u-1}(T_u | y_u) \right], \Sigma_u \right\}, \tag{11}$$

where $\Sigma_u$ and $\Gamma_u$ are given by (5) and (6). Recursive application of this formula then gives (3) for any $u \leq t$. For $u > t$, the mean and the variance of the beliefs are only affected by addition of independent increments of tax parameter changes. ∎

**Proof of Proposition 2.** Note that (5) implies that $\Sigma_{t-1}(y_{t-1}, 1)^T = 0$, and hence

$$(\Sigma_{t-1} + S_t)(y_t, 1)^T = \Sigma_{t-1}(y_t, 1)^T + S_t(y_t, 1)^T$$

$$= \Sigma_{t-1}(y_{t-1}, 1)^T + \Sigma_{t-1}(\Delta y_t, 0)^T + S_t(y_t, 1)^T$$

$$= \Sigma_{t-1}(\Delta y_t, 0)^T + S_t(y_t, 1)^T.$$

Given (7), both elements of $S_t(y_t, 1)^T$ are strictly positive. As a result, if $|\Delta y_t|$ is small enough, the same sign pattern applies to the elements of $(\Sigma_{t-1} + S_t)(y_t, 1)^T$, and hence, by (6), also the elements of $\Gamma_t$. ∎